To
Mr & Mrs. B. People,
Happy reading.
Troggy.

LAUGH AND SIGH

LAUGH AND SIGH

FROGGY

VANTAGE PRESS
New York

FIRST EDITION

Published by Vantage Press, Inc.
516 West 34th Street, New York, New York 10001

Manufactured in the United States of America
ISBN: 0-533-10889-6

Library of Congress Catalog Card No.: 93-94959

0 9 8 7 6 5 4 3 2 1

To 185 officers and men of the HMS *Exmouth* who so gallantly gave their lives in the Second World War. Without their wit and good humour to remember them by, this book would never have been written.

Contents

Sad Mechanics	1
Honest Horace, the Con Man	2
One Less	5
Pinch Bank	9
A World Doomed	11
Dorset	13
Goals, Goals, Goals	17
Poor Cow	19
Why Worry	21
How Chef Won the War	23
Made to Measure	25
Ignored at Chelsea	27
Bright Sparks	29
Poole, Dorset	31
The Enemy	33
Stress	35
Poor Dentist	37
Wanted—£10,000 Reward	39
Fact or Fiction	41
Heaven Bound	42
The Loner	45
The Poor Ruddy Gasman	49
Requiem for a Pet	51
Number 10	53
It's a Dog's Life	55
Cowboy Supreme	57
Bits and Pieces	60
Life Eternal	63
Wanton Cruelty	65
Thoughts of Summer	67
Destination Scrap-yard	69
New Life	71
Youth	73
The Huntsman's Horn	75

The Motor	77
No Claims Bonus	79
The Flying Scotsman	80

LAUGH AND SIGH

HOPE
GARAGE
IN
OUT

Sad Mechanics

She was sick, very very sick,
Her headlights hung in pain.
A piston had gone through her side
And her crankshaft hung in vain.

She was so young; only three,
Could not have travelled far.
Her young life was full of spree,
Now the light had left her star.

They treated her quite gently
To relieve added pain.
Then replaced damaged parts
To help her start again.

Auto choke thrown right out,
By manual replaced;
Her little heart bursting life,
Then out through doors she raced.

Mechanics stood to wave good-bye,
Her exhaust purred them thanks.
Then suddenly all gave a sigh
As she got flattened by two tanks.

Honest Horace, the Con Man

Bank manager overdraft bars,
Showroom full of unsold cars.
Overcome eyes fill with tears,
Stony-broke after toiling years.

Man from tax decides to call,
Almost drives him up the wall.
Business now on the blink,
Scratches head, tries to think.

Ties rope to highest shelf,
Then decides to hang himself.
Jumps off desk in defeat,
To find he'd landed on his feet.

Having failed in that attempt,
Received large bill for unpaid rent.
He gave up in his sorrow,
To try something else tomorrow.

Jumped in car to end it all,
Built up speed and drove at wall.
Steering snapped before impact,
Ending up in hay well stacked.

Tried again he'd failed so far,
Attached hose to exhaust of car.
Started engine ran a minute,
Petrol out, he'd forgot to fill it.

Knowing now he was meant to live,
A look at showroom he would give.
Arriving back into the town,
Saw showroom burnt right down.

GOD FORGIVE ME
FOR BEING HONEST
HONEST HORACE CARE

Insurance cheque which he received,
Gave him hope, he felt relieved.
Paid off debts, now sleeps at night,
Dreaming of showroom he'd set alight.

One Less

Oh dear, oh dear, oh dear,
His heart is filled with fear.
The envelope to his address
Bore the letters O.H.M.S.

With ominous fear, looked inside.
Suddenly eyes popped open wide.
A deadly fright now takes hold,
Then all his blood goes very cold.

Reading aloud he starts exam,
Finds it's from that nice tax man
Asking for a massive figure,
Which each year gets bigger and bigger.

Sells his house: most prized chattel
Helping him to fight the battle.
Now that figure trebled in score
Gets up his nose; he can take no more.

This demand he cannot meet,
Then starts shaking from head to feet.
With big fat wife and fifteen kids,
Her in bed now another life gives.

He went outside, let out a shout,
Then finally blew his poor brains out.
Next day arrived on mat
Letter stating he owed no VAT.

He's paid too much came back on fax,
There'd been an error: he owed no tax.
This colossal figure on demand
Was given back to his dead hand.

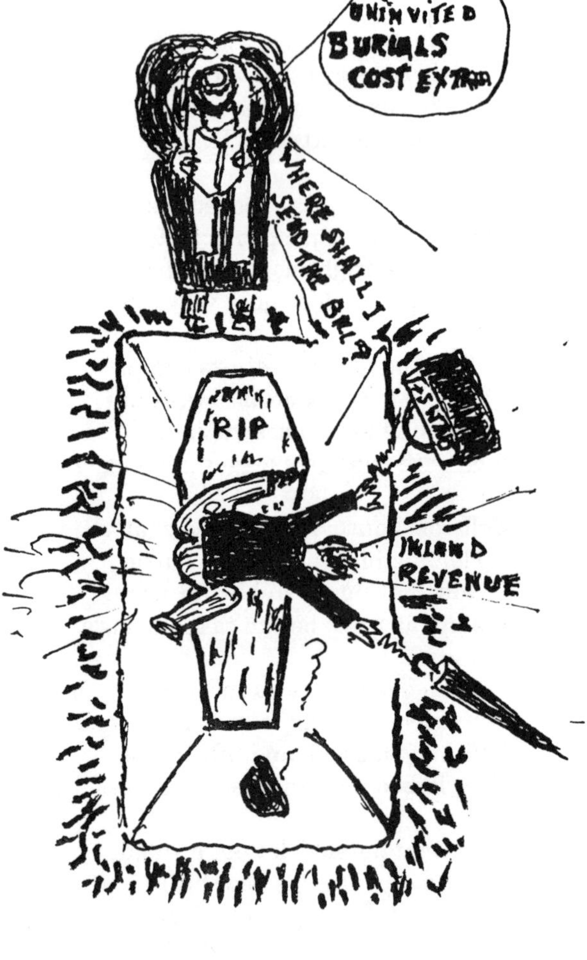
UNINVITED BURIALS COST EXTRA
WHERE SHALL I SEND THE BILL?
INLAND REVENUE

Funeral paid by the state
Cause massive rebate; arrived too late.
At grave-side poor tax-man wept,
His falling tears on coffin swept.

Emotions now beyond his call
His heart caved in; into grave did fall,
Which now proves beyond a doubt
Obliging tax-men are about.

I ONLY ASKED FOR A LOAN
LOANS
SECURITIES
PINCH BANK
PINCH BANK
BOSS
SEND AMBULANCE NEVER MIND MAKE IT A HEARSE
POLICE

Pinch Bank

Calling on bank manager to raise a loan,
Bill poured out his problems in one mighty moan.
Manager to soothe him with sympathy tried,
Leaned on Bill's shoulder and actually cried.

"You think you've got problems," he said with a sob,
"I've fiddled the till, now I'm losing my job."
Bill thought 'twas nice to show his concern,
Felt awfully low and cried in return.

Footsteps grew louder, manager raced to the door,
Slammed home the bolts and raced across floor.
"What's the panic?" Bill asked. "Fraud squad," he replied,
Dived through the window and immediately died.

Down came the door, they grabbed Bill tight,
Shackled him up in cell for the night.
He tried to explain the wrong man they'd got,
Told him to shut up or else he'd be shot.

Bill later released, let out on bail,
Suffering visions of lifetime in jail.
Before judge days later, he explained events,
Accepting the judgement, enjoying comments.

Judge said, "I'm sorry to court you've arrived,
I didn't know culprit through window had dived."
Bill later sued police for wrongful arrest,
Now he's counting the lolly stacked on his chest.

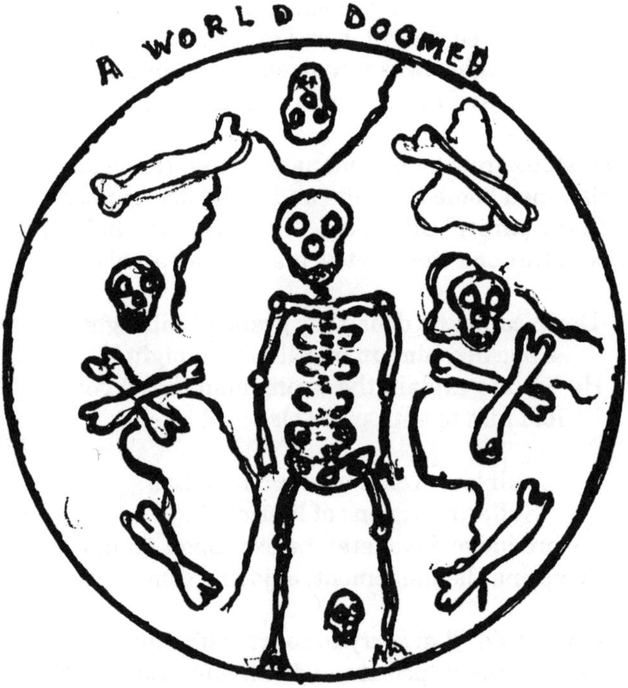
A WORLD DOOMED

A World Doomed

This modern world to doom races,
Destroying life without basis.
Land, seas, rivers now polluted,
Human anger so deep-rooted.

Atom stations increase in power,
Leaking radiation, fall-out shower.
Populations boom and boom,
Soon there'll be no standing room.

Earth destroyed for monetary gain
Whilst people starve for want of grain.
Money spent on war and rockets,
Better sent to Third World pockets.

Unemployment grows and grows,
Creating spite as crime well shows.
Politicians our money devour,
Raising taxes by the hour.

Science now has gone too far,
With babies made inside a jar.
Populations must be controlled,
Two a family, no more enrolled.

If man stood still for time to think,
Then made self-gain, go on the blink.
He'd end up with the right solution,
A cleaner world with no pollution.

Surely man is not so blind
As not to see what he'll leave behind.
He has the answer in his head,
If not in cesspit we'll end up dead.

He's thinned the layer in the roof,
Melting ice caps produce the proof.
With ultra-violet we're bombarded,
From factories—poisons left unguarded.

Nothing living on this earth
Will create another birth.
Now you know what is in store,
Try cleaning up this oozing sore.

Dorset

I first saw lovely Dorset
When I was then a boy.
Playing in its countryside
Exuberant with joy.

Then in my youth I travelled far,
The oceans I did ride.
My mind still dwelling on
The Dorset countryside.

No matter where I travelled
In countries old and new,
I saw nothing to match
This Dorset view.

The Dorset lakes I still adore,
Closed in by a sandy shore.
Lovely beaches on which to laze
Whilst admiring summer's haze.

There's Evening Hill, a beauty spot
With a view out to sea.
Brownsea Isle right opposite,
A gorgeous place to be.

The waters ripple far below
Supporting sailing boats.
All colours of the rainbow
As their sails pass to and fro.

I sat there watching sunset
As it settled in the west
Outlining Dorset's landscape
With Corfe Castle in its crest.

Above my head the seagulls screech.
I scatter them some bread.
Then from a nearby branch
A squirrel nods his head.

UPHAM FC
GOALS
UPHAM FC
SNOOZE
The Gray

Goals, Goals, Goals

At final whistle to dressing room race
Followed by trainer at equal fast pace.
Manager follows, lets out a roar,
"Six goals between you—what a good score."

"You've set quite a record all on your own,
With my sense of humour, how can I moan.
I asked you to score, that task you have met;
I meant into their goal, not your own ruddy net."

"Those points against us will all now be stacked,
I've no more to say—you're all ruddy-well sacked."

DUCK POND
SILAGE

Poor Cow

Farmer Johnson had an awkward cow,
Wouldn't give milk, no way no how.
Worked her mechanically, also by hand,
Played her music from the village band.

He called in vets from far and wide
Who coaxed her lovingly and stroked her hide.
With curious eyes she turned her head,
Gave a mighty kick and cleared the shed.

Decision was made, she'd end up as beef.
She let out a sigh and thought of the grief.
Wisdom was needed, her eyes opened wide;
Finally decided she'd stick to her hide.

Lonely she stayed in the shed all that night,
Waking next morning with hope and delight.
She'd made up her mind, she wanted to live,
Instead of meat, warm milk she would give.

Now came the time to give of her best,
Wore out machine, hands needed a rest.
Upsetting the farmer, no milk had he got,
Took her outside to one deadly shot.

Her carcass purchased, travels world-wide;
Turned into shoes made from her hide.
So if when walking, your feet start to sweat,
Think of poor cow and the end that she met.

CWT
WOE IS ME
CWT
CWT
TONS
WORRIES
PROBLEMS

Why Worry

Problems, worries, aggravation.
The mind thinks, and having thought
Thinks on—and on—and on.
Still no solution.

People can be most unkind.
Think harder, think harder, mind.
Still no clear decision
From mind's distorted vision.

Wishful thinking, waste of time,
Memory gets out of rhyme.
Concentrate more and more:
Worries, problems, such a bore.

Now place mind some years hence,
Present problems not so tense.
They're forgotten with the sorrow.
Now there's room for more tomorrow.

The moral to this is—worry can
Kill you. You'll die one day anyway.
So why worry at all?

How Chef Won the War

Poor old chef cooking his bangers,
Suppressing fears and hidden angers,
Decided his effort needed direction,
Invented a weapon defying radar detection.

With bangers fresh, soft to his feel
Came a weapon from which enemies reel.
Frying them thro' really stone hard,
Stacking them up yard by the yard.

Swiping the cook-house with his new stunt,
Jumped into seat and drove to the front.
Using his frying pan held as a bat,
Banging enemy tanks, laying 'em flat.

So proud was his C.O. he made him a medal
Shaped as a banger from enemy scrap metal.
No one can stop him, no one gets a rest,
Parading around with medal on his chest.

SWAG

Made to Measure

Recessions come, recessions go,
He sews away like Mighty Mo.
Demand for suits will not last,
So he pushes up prices very fast.

With measuring tape on shoulders bent,
He stitches away all hours God sent.
His phone now rings, one order passed,
Decision made, a question asked.

Dawn arrived, he'd had no sleep,
Loss of business makes him weep.
Passing years have left their mark,
He's tiring fast and things look dark.

Then came the day the blow was struck,
His order book ran out of luck.
Now David since his trade began
Took instant dislike to poor tax-man.

He had a hobby, he loved to cook,
Instead of food 'twas takings book.
He staked his savings on the desk
Then bagged the lot as he thought best.

A glossy brochure in his hand
Of golden beaches and hotels grand.
His door flew open, they knocked him cold
And parted with his pot of gold.

When he came to, he thought it funny,
David hadn't lost his money.
What they'd grabbed, they had got
Theatrical money from an auction lot.

"THE BLADE"
PRESENTED BY NATURE.

Ignored at Chelsea

How much we take for granted
That little blade of grass.
We almost ignore it
As on our way we pass.

Out in all weathers
Without a roof at all.
Sometimes buried
By a deep snow fall.

Mother Nature's carpet
On which we run and walk,
Laid out in shades of green
For us to sit and talk.

Grazed on by animals,
Some chewed up in cud.
When protecting from the wind
A small flowering bud.

Oh, blade amongst billions,
May you one day find
A peaceful place of honour
With trophies close behind.

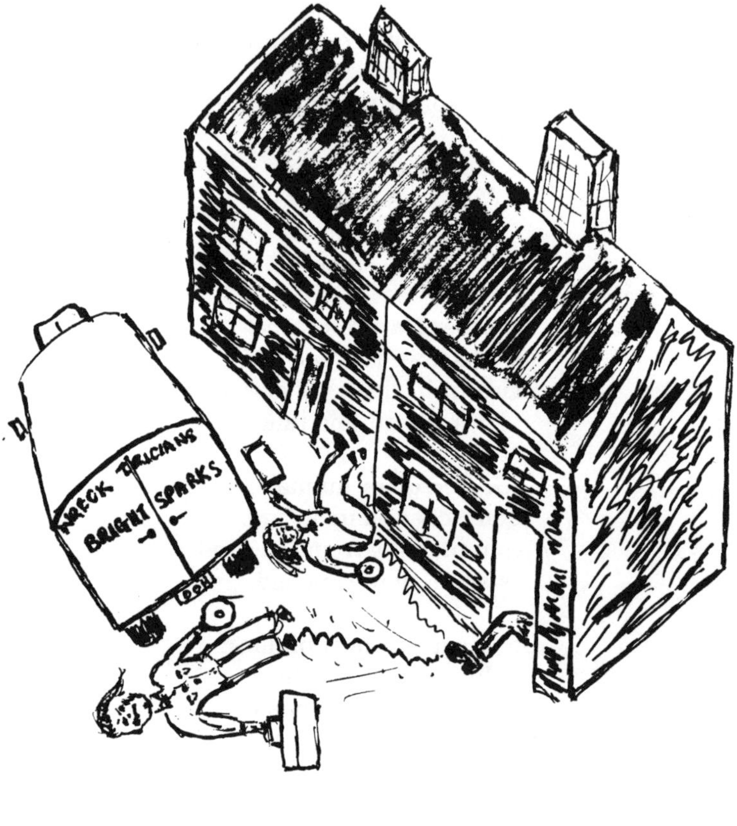
WRECK TRICIANS
BRIGHT SPARKS

Bright Sparks

With order in hand they set out in van
To rewire a house according to plan.
Door was unlocked with no-one in sight,
So deposited tools and portable light.

Sent up to attic one bright spark,
Who fell through ceiling because it was dark.
Damaged piano as plaster fell down,
Made carpet look white, 'twas originally brown.

Whipped out old wiring, sockets and all,
Tore up floor boards and damaged a wall.
Drilled through the main, which flooded the room,
Shattered TV with head of a broom.

Householder returned with frown on his brow,
Then started to kick up a fearsome row.
His language as such you'd read in no book,
Then almost collapsed when he took second look.

They tried to explain as they held him at bay,
Rewiring a house was done in this way.
"My home you've wrecked, just look at the mess."
Showed him the order—'twas not his address.

Poole, Dorset

Citizens with pride renown
Speak with love of old Poole Town.
Mixing buildings of the past
With modern structures built to last.

Ships arrive from o'er the world,
Showing countries on flags unfurled.
Near the harbour by the quay
Bata and park for revelry.

Ancient places to explore,
Old English pubs add up the score.
Makes one wonder with a doubt
What "Old Harry" left about.

So much history in this port,
Making an ideal resort.
Is it any wonder we're so vain
When visitors all come back again.

The Enemy

Oh, enemy; oh, enemy,
I have you in my sights.
I know you not for what you are
With all your wrongs and rights.

A mother, wife or girlfriend
No doubt you have back home.
You may not want to fight in war,
Yet I can't let you roam.

I have a right to kill you
As you would kill me back,
So say good-bye to Mother
As I drop you in your track.

DO YOU WANT ANYTHING ELSE?
YES PLEASE!
WE WILL NOT BE HERE
THEY WANT YOU TOMORROW

Stress

Let the eyelids drop,
Lay back and switch off.
Drift into dreamland,
Live the life of a toff.

In a tropical breeze
Neath swaying palm trees,
Resting each eye
Neath cloudless blue sky.

Full glass in hand,
You relax on warm sand.
Now comes the sting,
The phone starts to ring.

Your startled reaction
Causes contraction.
Your heart gets a shock,
Now you're mortuary stock.

So enjoy life today,
Don't throw it away.
Take a rest between work
And don't be a jerk.

DENTAL COLLEGE
DRILLING AND EXTRACTION
TAUGHT

Poor Dentist

With knee on his chest, his mouth open wide,
"This will not hurt," the dentist lied.
With eyeball to eyeball, white coat on top,
Chair began shaking and finally did drop.

Pinning him down in case he should run,
Rolling on floor the battle had begun.
No quarter was given as they belted away,
Furniture smashed, and building did sway.

Then back into chair with one mighty haul,
The dentist had got him with a throw and a fall.
Down came the forceps, he dodged and they missed,
So close came their mouths they actually kissed.

Dawn was now breaking, he would not submit,
Put half nelson on dentist, his jaw he did hit.
With wide-eyed delight and forceps in hand
Extracted his teeth, white, even and grand.

Prostrate on his chair, poor dentist remains,
As patient runs off with ill-gotten gains.
His surgery smashed, he's practising still,
Digging up roads with a pneumatic drill.

"HELP"
POLICE
WANTED

Wanted—£10,000 Reward

Tall oaks and pines no longer stand,
Lay splintered, uprooted over the land.
Dust now settled where kennel once stood,
'Twas made of concrete instead of wood.

He travelled at speed, faster than sound;
Stopped with a jerk that trembled the ground.
Black, shiny, playful; a beautiful pet,
He's only a puppy, strong and well set.

As nature would have it, one day he grew up,
Now even worse than when just a pup.
With innocent face, mine he will lick,
Asking forgiveness—should be back in nick.

No prison can hold him, he chews through the bars,
Chases all coppers, bursts tyres on their cars.
Races back home, sits as quiet as a dove;
What can I do? He's the dog that I love.

"FACT OR FICTION"

Fact or Fiction

When God made the world, he injected it with billions and billions of spirits, out of which came the largest of mammals, the tiniest of insects, the tallest trees to the smallest plants and everything that has life.

The number of spirits remain constant despite the creatures, which become extinct—i.e., when a dinosaur died, his spirit could have moved to a tiny insect; when the insect dies, his spirit could move to a man.

All living things go through this never-ending process. Nothing is destroyed. Fungi lives on dead matter.

Therefore, whatever pain you cause in this life, you will get back in the next. So if you're thinking of kicking the cat, do it gently—it could be you next time around.

So watch it, mate!

Heaven Bound

Paddy Murphy, big and strong,
Did nothing right and everything wrong.
His voice was loud, his manner rough,
Oh, boy! Oh, boy! Was this man tough!

Paddy set out with his juggernaut,
Through foreign lands, bandit fraught.
On mountain passes he goes careering,
Flags waving, crowds all cheering.

Bandits try to block his way,
Rockets, machine guns on camels sway.
Mountain peaks miles ahead,
Sun bears down, poor Paddy's red.

Paddy's mouth lets out a roar,
Shattering mountains by the score.
All obstructions within the sound
Now levelled to the ground.

Load delivered, Paddy turns,
Picking up speed, engine burns.
Through bandits he drives gaily,
Cracking heads with his shillalah.

Ice and snow on roads appear,
Paddy shows no sign of fear.
Takes in deep breaths, breaths on track
Bringing normal surface back.

Many countries left behind,
Paddy finds his peace of mind.
Chewing hard upon his gum,
Thinking of Guinness laced with rum.

MURP
GUINESS
PAT 1

By this time brake shoes torn,
Parks his truck on hill well worn.
Then jumped out to have a wee,
Truck rolls forward and ends his spree.

Back at base they all did mourn
Paddy Murphy and showed no scorn.
At the gates St. Peter chuckled,
Paddy arrived with his winkle buckled.

The Loner

Oh, this lonely world,
This lonely, lonely world.
If only I had a friend,
My loneliness would end.

I eat, sleep, and walk alone,
No one cares to say "Good day."
So I wander on my way.

I see people pass me by,
There's just the earth, the sun, the sky.
Oh, will this never end.
Please, God, send me a friend.

I walk for miles, my eyes to see
Flowers beautiful, and beyond a tree
A sparrow flies from branch to branch,
Chased by another. Perhaps romance.

Children's voices, laughing, crying,
Couples walking, talking, sighing.

Oh, sweet-smelling flowers,
Here I'll sit, and stay for hours
Watching, listening
Till the stars start glistening.

It's getting chilly, must go home,
To my bed I must roam.
I push my key into the door,
No one greets me any more.

The room is cold, the meter empty.
No one this life could envy.
In dark I must, I must look;
I think I've lost my pension book.

A loving husband was my Dave,
He sleeps now in his grave.
Wish I could afford the fare,
I'd catch a bus, I'm welcome there.

The Frog

The Poor Ruddy Gasman

With crowbar raised he made a pass,
Missed his target and hit the gas.
His mouth fell open, his fag fell out,
He didn't have much time to shout.

The road blew up, the house came down,
A bang was heard all over town.
The gasman came and gave a scream,
A bigger mess he'd never seen.

Emergency, emergency, a gas main has blown,
Out amongst the hazards the gasman stands alone.
Traffic pouring down on him, this he must command,
Stepping back just in time as a truck whips off his hand.

Brave and still undaunted back to the road he goes,
Then along came a juggernaut, which ran across his toes.
The wind and rain came driving on, but he bravely stood his site,
When a branch from up above his bare head did smite.

They buried him across the main, the spot where he did fall,
Then had to dig him up again to rest beside the wall.
The wind blew hard, the wall came down and landed on his head,
A doctor passing by announced the poor blighter dead.

So look out, all you drivers, when belting in the rain,
For the poor ruddy gasman who's looking for his main.

"IN MEMORY OF TROTTY"
"CHIHUAHUA"
"LITTLE BODY BIG HEART"

Requiem for a Pet

How sad, how very very sad;
My greatest friend has died.
I've known the love and trust he gave,
So I cried, and cried, and cried.

I dug his grave beneath his tree,
The one he loved the most.
Near where we used to walk,
My friend, my love, my host.

His tiny body rests in peace,
His bark I'll hear no more.
A lonely world he's left behind
With a broken heart so sore.

Man places love and trust in his pet,
He reaps back tenfold what he gives.
Such returns from man he'll never get
No matter how long he lives.

Nu

Maggie screame
Animals fright
Security to h
Pointing gun

Advancing swif
When out throug
Carrying whi
A victory for E

They fell on
Then marched
In his cel
Watching hang

Petitions arr
Crowds stret
Public opin
Why to To

Maggie o
Enrolled him
Now he wa
In charge of pant

It's a Dog's Life

Awakened from slumber, hooked on to lead,
Taken for walkies to meet bosses need.
Start to run forward, get a pull on the neck;
If boss keeps it up, I'll be a physical wreck.

Now that we're walking, I'll soon need a tree,
I'm all right, I can bend at the knee.
He's looking awkward, I know what he needs,
Looks over his shoulder then slyly pees.

I'm getting thirsty, I know he is too,
Usually in barn now with no more ado.
At last we're turning, bee-line for the pub
Looking exhausted, like a worn-out wheel hub.

Squats on his stool whilst breathing re-found,
"Pint for me and half for the hound."
Chap sitting next asks, "What breed has it got?"
Boss looks at me, "It's got all the lot."

I show him my teeth, get a pat on the head,
If he'd tapped any harder, I'd be ruddy-well dead.
My stomach was pounding for something to eat;
Got thrown a crisp but no blooming meat.

Boss knocking back pints fell off his stool.
I was embarrassed and felt quite a fool.
Getting him home will be my next job,
I'll just have to drag him, the drunken big slob.

Collaring his neck on the end of my lead,
Then dragging him home 'twas my only good deed.
His Missus was waiting, rolling pin in her hand,
Screaming at sight, then pin on him slammed.

Must find him shelter, put him up for the night,
Dragged him in kennel so he'd be out of sight.
Went back to house, crept quietly upstairs,
Got into bed with his wife unawares.

Snuggled up in blanket, lovely and warm
Slept like an angel and woke up at dawn.
Raced to the kennel, looked at the heap
Snoring its head off in deep drunken sleep.

Out came his Missus, full bucket in hand;
Hit him with contents, I thought it was grand.
Thro' catching pneumonia he died the next day.
I was treated as guilty and given away.

Now I am happy, I have a good home;
Lovely big garden for me just to roam.
I ride around in comfort in ladies posh car,
Not bad for a mongrel renamed "The Tsar."

Cowboy Supreme

Phoned up the builder for house him to build,
He laid down the rubble with concrete did shield.
Stacked up his bricks, timber and all,
Then started to lay first bricks of the wall.

Built up to eight feet four walls to stand force,
Then suddenly realised he'd forgotten damp course.
But being a plodder he reached roof-top height
Then acted like man who'd had a big fright.

He'd bricked in the windows, also the doors;
Forgotten to lay joists to hold up the floors.
After much trial-and-error corrected the faults,
Called in with his bill and grinned at results.

Why did I pay him? I'm wondering still,
Such a massive amount sticks in the gill.
When he was leaving, slammed shut the door,
House began shaking as roof met the floor.

The one wall left standing at thirty degrees
Slowly collapsed when caught in the breeze.
I took it quite hard like a smack on the jaw:
Knew I'd been done, so called in the law.

Went to the court for trial to take place:
Looked at defendant—'twas not the same face.
He said, "I'm the builder employed for the job
But contracted out to fellow called Slob.

"He hasn't been seen, never paid me the cheque,
So I can't be responsible for the idiot's wreck."
I parted in sorrow being quids down the pan:
Made to pay costs of this horrible man.

SHIFT YER RUBBLE GUV!

That was too much but there's more on the way,
Must pay for the rubble to be taken away.
You may be surprised who turned up for the job:
'Twas that twisting, conniving cowboy called Slob.

Bits and Pieces

Don't ban the bomb, ban sex; same effect
but more painful.

H.M.S. *Vernon* during war: "Halt! Who goes there?"
(answer) "Vernon wren."
(reply) "Advance, virgin wren, and be circumcised."

He that speaks with false tongue will never be
master of his own mind.

Young paratrooper to sergeant: "Suppose it doesn't open?"
Sergeant: "Then bring it back and we'll change it."

How to make love gently: watch the hedge hogs.

How to be good in bed: keep practising.

Customer with part exchange car: "I can't remember
the name of its colour."
Salesman: "I can, it's rust."

"Hello, Harry, why are you laughing?"
"Well, mother-in-law has just borrowed the car,
and I'm holding the master brake cylinder."

Paddy the yachtsman set out to sail the Atlantic but
forgot to take his yacht. Amen.

A man with troubled mind who isolates himself from
others is like a sinking ship; only one way to go.

"War": Living today, hoping to see tomorrow.

He that laughs last make a happy corpse.

Don't blame your mother for your bad looks—
wait until you see her mother.

"If you were my husband, I'd shoot you."
"Madam, if you were my wife, I'd supply the bullets."

"Bob, my office is freezing; can I borrow your heater?"
"Of course, Jack, I'll send her in."

Life Eternal

From the cradle where we weep
Time starts passing whilst we sleep.
Given love and great devotion
Naught can stop this aging motion.

Happy childhood being gay
All seems wonderful as we play.
Youth arrives with its problems,
Unsure, doubtful, sometimes doldrums.

Learning, writing, adding, spelling,
Homework tiring and compelling.
We start to see so much of life,
Self-assurance, hope and strife.

Combating life in the raw,
Which when younger we never saw.
Striving in this world of greed,
Hoping marriage will succeed.

Child arrives bringing pleasure;
Infant-minding is our leisure.
Ambitious father bent on earning,
Saving hard for youngster's learning.

Bills pile up through the door,
Love and patience on child pour.
Life repeats the same old cycle,
Child, youth and marriage title.

Then we go onto old age;
Years showing their rampage.
Until we reach three score and ten,
Peace and quiet our only yen.

The Frog

Wanton Cruelty

The sky is my playground, cloudless and blue;
I see countryside with its marvellous hue.
Sheep in the meadows, cows on the graze,
I'm a bird and downwards I gaze.

My freedom is such all trees are my home,
I sing to the humans as I fly and I roam.
With dog there's a man, gun shoulder hung;
I am his target—with hot pellets I'm stung.

My eyes cannot see, my wings flap in vain,
Torturingly falling, racked through with pain.
I'd hoped when I sang to my trill he'd rejoice,
Now I am blind, without even a voice.

Barbed wire tears my flesh, all things have gone dark,
I know I am dying as sharp teeth follow bark.
God made me for you, man, to watch and be heard,
I was beautiful, I was a bird.

Thoughts of Summer

A gentle breeze breathes on my face,
Along the beach my footsteps pace.
A piece of driftwood in my track,
I pick it up and throw it back.

The gentle movement of the sand
Lifts through my toes; the feeling's grand.
Pin-pricked lights from a liner shine,
Sailing at dusk on a navigable line.

A seagull lays upon its back
With broken wings as if hit with flak.
Jetsam washed to high-tide mark,
Seaweed shells and bits of bark.

Overhead in a darkening sky
Seagulls screech whilst flying by.
How I'd love on this beach to stay,
Must home to bed for work next day.

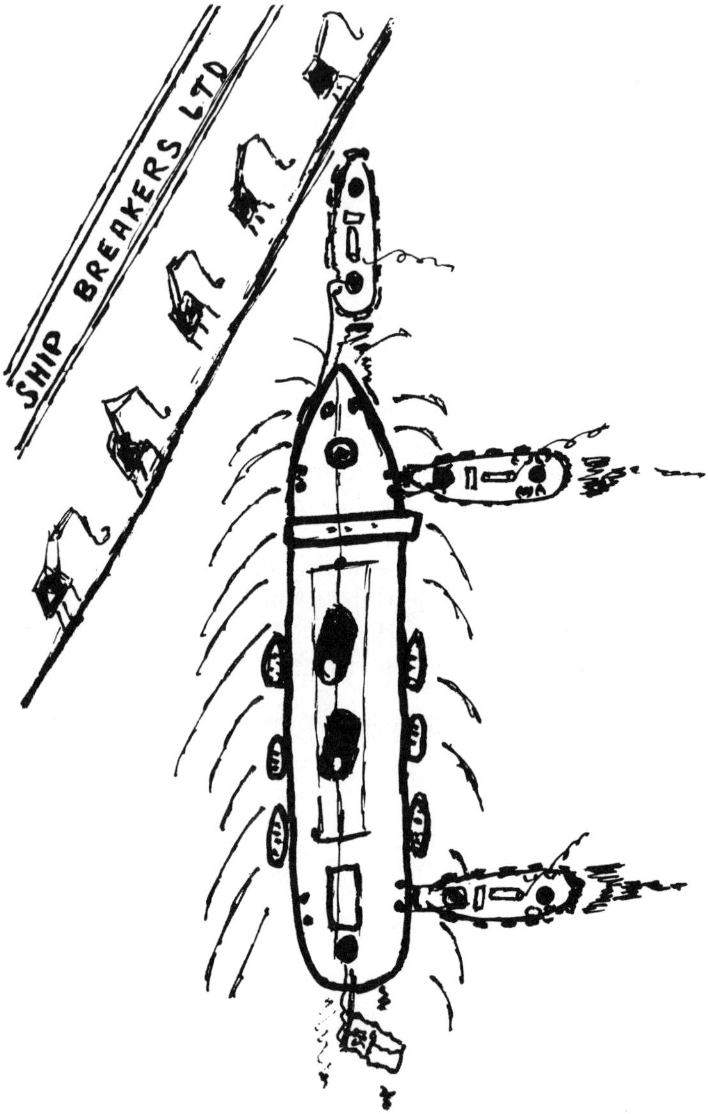
SHIP BREAKERS LTD

Destination Scrap-yard

Gathering clouds predict the rain,
Storm-tossed seas appear again.
Hull scarred by rust and dent
From years of cruising pleasure-bent.

Captain calm and duty-bound
Listens to hull's creaking sound.
Another day, perhaps tomorrow,
Harbour safe and saved from sorrow.

All that night she battled on
Through raging seas, weighed by the ton.
Howling winds increased her roll,
Hissing at her very soul.

Then at dawn land appeared,
Dead on course, up harbour steered.
There to rest beside the wharf,
Saved from the cruel sea's wrath.

From his bridge the captain walks,
Meeting breakers having talks.
No sound of laughter from within,
Acetylene cutting will soon begin.

"I've been your master thirty years,
Please forgive these last few tears.
Good-bye, my friend, I cherished thee,
The last bell hath tolled for you and me."

New Life

Spring, spring, spring,
You beautiful season,
Bringing new life
By God's very good reason.

Mother Nature puts on her show,
Layers of green, flowers that glow.
Young birds on the wing,
Listen how sweetly they sing.

Breathe the air
It too is new,
Sweetened by flowers
Kissed by the dew.

Watch the lambs romp about,
The field mouse as he looks in doubt.
Then from the sky there dives a hawk,
And nature allows a little squawk.

Sense the feeling of new awakening,
So much life after hibernating.
Watch the sunlight through the trees
Where shadows move, helped by the breeze.

Look across the meadows wide,
New foliage for your guide.
See all this and much more too;
God gave this and it's all for you.

Youth

Have I the courage to travel,
Life's problems yet to unravel.
On this the road to my destiny
Yet seek in passing revelry.

Should I choose then turn back,
Forever my brain to rack.
Ne'er to find tranquility,
'Twas this a possibility?

Then should I see the tunnel's end,
Look far beyond and see a friend.
To talk of achievements made
Afore earth slips from spade.

The Huntsman's Horn

The wily fox, with ears so sharp
In the distance heard hounds bark.
He knew the hunt was on today;
Intelligence told him, get away.

Autumn leaves had had their fall,
Earth covered brown overall.
Coat matching his surrounding,
Huntsman's horns within his sounding.

Now was the time to use his wits,
Dodge those hounds with clever tricks.
He knew the land so very well,
The murky brook with the musty smell.

He took off in a fast, long stride
To where the brook was very wide.
Left his scent on a high stacked heap,
Then went back and took a leap.

He dived nose-down into the brook
And swam along it like a duck.
The hounds came on and lost his scent,
Returning home with heads all bent.

RIP

The Motor

Came the wheel—man's invention
To remove the strain and added tension.
Then from the earth came the ore,
So man made more and more.

He then learned how to bend the metal;
Eventually he made a pedal.
To this he added a rotor,
A few more bits and he had a motor.

He poured them out like shelling peas,
Then forgot his feet and knees.
He used to walk across the plains,
Through the valleys, and down the lanes.

Now he drives where he used to walk.
He can't smell the flowers or hear birds talk.
He kills himself off in his race for leisure:
The bills pile up and he calls it pleasure.

There's too many models to suit his modes,
Too many motors and not enough roads.
He tried to start walking, lost the use of his limbs,
Fell off the pavement and collected his wings.

He took his last ride to a permanent rest
In a black Rolls-Royce with a wreath on his chest.
So come on, you drivers, keep your legs fit and trim
Or the same fate for you that happened to him.

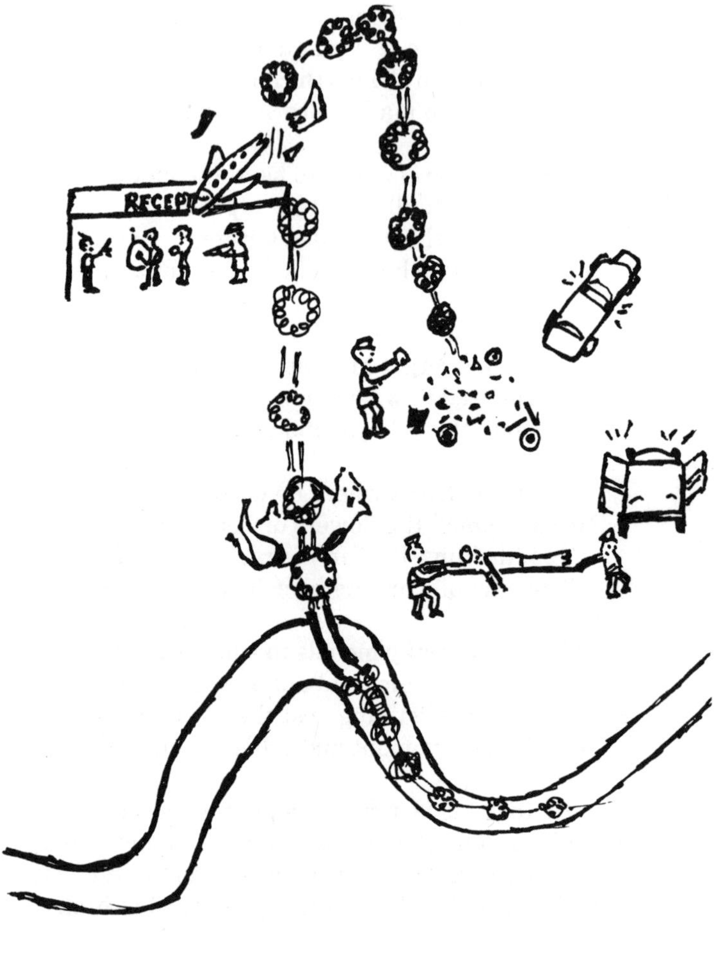
RECEPT

No Claims Bonus

Extolling its virtues as he stood at the bar,
Johnny kept talking about his new car.
He knocked back his whiskey, one over the eight,
Jumped in the car and tried to drive straight.

Mounting the pavement time and again,
Splattering blood, which poured down the drain.
He eased down to ninety to take an S-bend,
Bounced off a cow and began to ascend.

Hit the tail of a plane coming in to land,
Which crashed through reception and the welcoming band.
Johnny landed quite awkward, his head hit the ground;
From his wide open mouth came a gurgling sound.

With speed and efficiency the police did arrive
And seemed quite sorry to find him alive.
Sewn up in stitches from toes to his head,
Appearing in court when he ought to be dead.

The car he had taken without owner consent
Was twisted, distorted, and certainly bent.
He wasn't insured, had no licence to drive,
Now wished himself dead instead of alive.

The judge said to Johnny, "You're not insane:
Thirty years hard, and you'll pay for the plane."
Sweat from his labour through his pores hoose
As he goes on repenting his day on the booze.

The Flying Scotsman

He revved up the engine then let go the brakes,
Grabbed at the column and then got the shakes.
Climbed to five thousand, did a loop and a roll,
Got into a stall that was hard to control.

Put nose at deep angle, gave engine the gun,
Pulled out of the dive with seconds to run.
Went into cloud that was nearing the ground,
Giving church steeple a horrible pound.

Looking back, saw wheels stuck on the spire,
Now had to make landing, his only desire.
Keeping his cool he trimmed up the tail,
Then ran into storm of withering hail.

With compass kaput and dials on the blink;
What to do now, he sat back to think.
Fog moved in quickly obliterating ground,
Engine started making a loud banging sound.

Wings which were buckled started to sing,
Doing a dance like the Scots highland fling.
As fuel gauge showed empty, he'd hazard a guess
With what he had left, onwards he'd press.

Later in day came clear sky to land,
Looking for runway could only see sand.
A tank from some army was belting away,
Pot-holing his kite—it wasn't his day.

Jock, using his nut, tried to turn back,
Flew into his rudder, blown off by flak.
Belly-landing on sand, Jock had survived,
When hot on his heels some Arabs arrived.

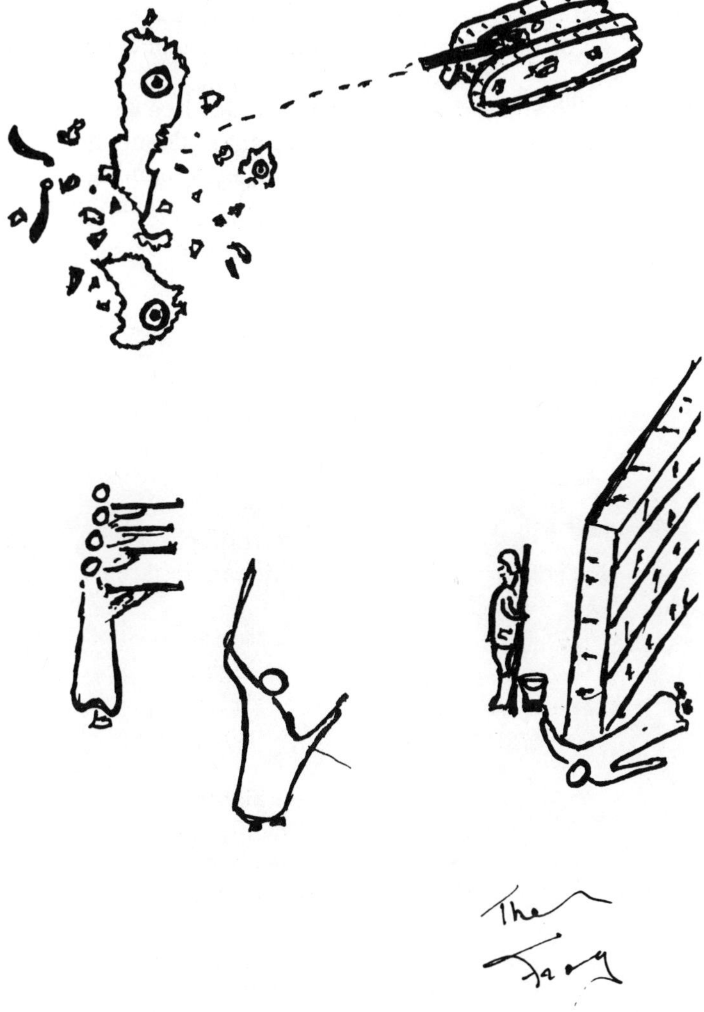

They charged him with spying, put his back to the wall,
Facing firing squad from where he would fall.
Rifles were raised, came the order, “Take aim,”
A brave Scot like Jock made no protest claim.

The noise that he heard sounded like shot,
And the seat of his pants became suddenly hot.
The sound of a jet with engines screaming
Made him wake up—he’d only been dreaming.